3/0/2

Team Spirit

THE PHILADELPHIA EAGLES

BY

MARK STEWART

Content Consultant
Jason Aikens
Collections Curator
The Professional Football Hall of Fame

NORWOOD HOUSE PRESS
CHICAGO, ILLINOIS

Norwood House Press
P.O. Box 316598
Chicago, Illinois 60631

For information regarding Norwood House Press, please visit our website at:
www.norwoodhousepress.com or call 866-565-2900.

All photos courtesy AP/Wide World Photos, Inc. except the following:
Bowman Gum, Inc. (7 bottom, 16, 30, 31 right, 38 & 43);
National Chickle (14, 34 left & 37 top); Topps, Inc. (18, 20, 21, 35 & 40); Author's
collection (9 & 14).
Special thanks to Topps, Inc.

Editor: Mike Kennedy
Designer: Ron Jaffe
Project Management: Black Book Partners, LLC.

Special thanks to: Steve Hynes and Laura Peabody.

Library of Congress Cataloging-in-Publication Data

Stewart, Mark.
  The Philadelphia Eagles / by Mark Stewart ; content consultant Jason
Aikens.
    p. cm. -- (Team spirit)
  Summary: "Presents the history, accomplishments and key personalities of
the Philadelphia Eagles football team. Includes timelines, quotes, maps,
glossary and websites"--Provided by publisher.
  Includes bibliographical references and index.
  ISBN-13: 978-1-59953-007-9 (library edition : alk. paper)
  ISBN-10: 1-59953-007-4 (library edition : alk. paper) 1. Philadelphia
Eagles (Football team)--History--Juvenile literature. I. Aikens, Jason. II.
Title. III. Series.
  GV956.P44S84 2006
  796.332'640974811--dc22
                                              2005033118

Manufactured in the United States of America.

COVER PHOTO: The Philadelphia Eagles rejoice after
intercepting an opponent's pass in 2002.

Table of Contents

SPORTS WORDS & VOCABULARY WORDS: In this book, you will find many words that are new to you. You may also see familiar words used in new ways. The glossary on page 46 gives the meanings of football words, as well as "everyday" words that have special football meanings. These words appear in **bold type** throughout the book. The glossary on page 47 gives the meanings of vocabulary words that are not related to football. They appear in ***bold italic type*** throughout the book.

Meet the Eagles

The team is everything in football. Great stars may make amazing plays, but it takes 11 players working as one to be successful. When the Philadelphia Eagles *emerge* from their locker room, they are moving as one and thinking as one. Each player is focused on the job he must do, and trusts his teammates to do their jobs, too. This makes the Eagles a very difficult team to beat.

The Eagles have an extra advantage that many teams do not. The fans of Philadelphia are loud, proud, and emotional. When the Eagles play as a team, the stadium comes alive. If a player is not doing his job, the fans will tell him before the coach has a chance.

This book tells the story of the Eagles. They have won great victories and lost heartbreaking games. When they win, they win as a team. When they lose, they lose as a team, too. What else would you expect from a team that plays in the "City of Brotherly Love?"

Brian Dawkins is congratulated by teammates after intercepting a pass.

Way Back When

The people of Philadelphia love football. They have been playing and watching the game for more than 100 years. It has always been an important part of city life. In the early days of the **National Football League (NFL)**, one of the best teams was the Yellow Jackets, who played their home games in Philadelphia. During the *Great Depression* of the 1930s, the Yellow Jackets could not sell enough tickets to pay their players and make repairs to their stadium. They went out of business in 1931.

Philadelphia's football fans were very sad. One fan, a wealthy man named Bert Bell, decided to do something about it. He started a new NFL team, the Philadelphia Eagles. Bell chose this name because it was the symbol for the government's New Deal programs, which were designed to create jobs for the unemployed. The team was coached by his friend, Lud Wray. The star of the

Bert Bell (center) meets with other NFL owners. In 1946, he was elected commissioner of the NFL.

Rugged Steve Van Buren gave the Eagles a great running game.

STEVE VAN BUREN

team was a running back named Swede Hanson, who had gone to college at Philadelphia's Temple University.

The Eagles lost their first three games by scores of 56–0, 25–0, and 35–9—and finished their first season with only three wins. The Eagles lost a lot of games and a lot of money over the next few years, but Bell refused to give up on his team. He believed **professional** football would become a big sport one day, and he believed that his team could win a championship. The other owners in the NFL had great respect for Bell. They made him the league's **commissioner** in 1946.

The Eagles struggled through tough times, and began to build a good team during the mid 1940s. They had the NFL's best defense, as well as the game's best running back, Steve Van Buren. In 1948, the Eagles beat the Chicago Cardinals 7–0 in the **NFL Championship** game. In 1949, they beat the Los Angeles Rams 14–0 in the title game for their second NFL Championship. The Eagles wore the NFL crown again in 1960, when a team led by *veterans* Chuck Bednarik and Norm Van Brocklin surprised the Green Bay Packers 17–13 in a thrilling championship battle.

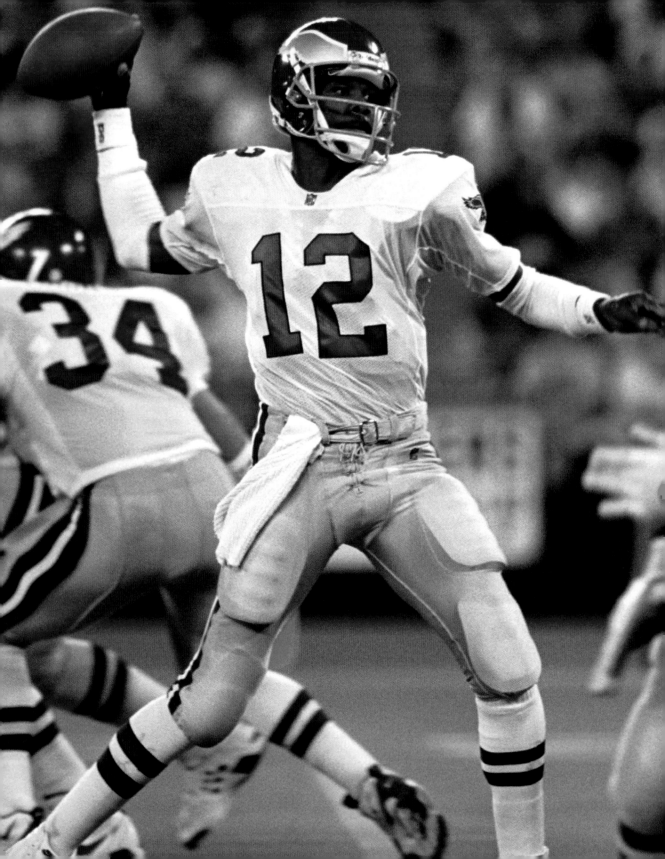

In 1969, millionaire Leonard Tose bought the Eagles for $16.1 million. No one had ever spent that much money on a professional team in any sport. In 1976, Tose hired Dick Vermeil to coach the team. Led by quarterback Ron Jaworski and running back Wilbert Montgomery, the Eagles flew to the top of the **standings** again in 1980, but lost to the Oakland Raiders in **Super Bowl** XV.

The team went through many ups and downs in the 1980s and 1990s. Some of the NFL's best players—including Reggie White and Randall Cunningham—played for the team during this time, but they could not get Philadelphia back to the Super Bowl. The team's new owner, Jeffrey Lurie, refused to give up. He wanted to bring the city another champion. He hired coach Andy Reid in 1999, and the two men *plotted* a strategy to help the Eagles soar again.

TOP: A souvenir pennant from Super Bowl XV.
LEFT: Randall Cunningham fires a pass downfield.
He was voted the league's best player twice when he played for the Eagles.

The Team Today

Like most good teams, the Eagles started winning by playing good defense. Their players were quick to recognize plays, and even quicker to react. They made good, hard tackles and helped each other out by swarming all over the man carrying the ball.

Playing better defense meant that the Eagles had more time to run plays on offense. In 2000, they made Donovan McNabb their quarterback, and started to put a lot of points on the board. McNabb had a strong arm, and was a very fast runner, too. If he saw that his receivers were covered, he could run for the yardage he needed. With defenses worried about McNabb, the Eagles' runners and receivers found that they had more space to do what they did best.

The Eagles have used this combination of a good team defense and a dangerous offense to become one of the best teams in the NFL. They have a chance to reach the Super Bowl almost every year.

Donovan McNabb runs for a first down.

Home Turf

The Eagles play their home games at Lincoln Financial Field. It opened in 2003, and everyone in Philadelphia loves the stadium. The players love the field, too. In their old stadium, the Eagles played on **artificial turf**. It was very hard. The playing surface in the new stadium is made of grass, which is much softer.

Every seat in the stands has a great view of the field. If you miss a play, you can watch a replay on one of the stadium's two giant video screens. One of the coolest things about the Eagles' home field are the giant steel eagle *talons* that sit high atop one end of the stadium.

LINCOLN FINANCIAL FIELD BY THE NUMBERS

- *The stadium seats 68,400 fans.*
- *It cost $512 million to build.*
- *The first sporting event held there was a soccer game between Manchester United and FC Barcelona.*
- *The Eagles played their first official game there against the Tampa Bay Buccaneers on September 8, 2003. They lost 17–0.*

The Eagles' stadium is one of the most modern in the NFL.

13

Dressed for Success

The Eagles' first uniforms were blue and white with bright yellow pants. Blue and yellow were Philadelphia's city colors. Bert Bell got so tired of hearing that his players were "yellow" (which means cowardly) that he switched to green and white. Later, the team added silver as a color. For many years, Philadelphia's helmet design had eagle wings spreading across the sides.

Today, the Eagles' colors are midnight green, white, and silver. They also use black for special occasions. For home games, they wear green jerseys and white pants. For road games, the Eagles wear white jerseys. The team's helmet features an eagle with a fearsome look in its eye.

JIM MacMURDO

LEFT: Lineman Jim MacMurdo poses in the Eagles uniform of the 1930s.
ABOVE: A souvenir button from the 1950s, when the Eagles included silver as a team color.

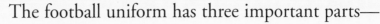

The football uniform has three important parts—
- Helmet
- Jersey
- Pants

Helmets used to be made out of leather, and they did not have facemasks—ouch! Today, helmets are made of super-strong plastic. The uniform top, or jersey, is made of thick fabric. It fits snugly around a player so that tacklers cannot grab it and pull him down. The pants come down just over the knees.

There is a lot more to a football uniform than what you see on the outside. Air can be pumped inside the helmet to give it a snug, padded fit. The jersey covers shoulder pads, and sometimes a rib-protector called a "flak jacket." The pants include pads that protect the hips, thighs, *tailbone*, and knees.

Football teams have two sets of uniforms—one dark and one light. This makes it easier to tell two teams apart on the field. Almost all teams wear their dark uniforms at home, and their light ones on the road.

Donovan McNabb's protective pads can be seen through his uniform as he prepares to pass.

We Won!

The road to the NFL Championship was long and hard for the Eagles. After many losing seasons, they finally built a winning team during the 1940s. The first step in the Eagles' journey came when they hired Alfred "Greasy" Neale. Neale was a very smart coach who demanded that his players give their best at all times.

Neale's favorite player was Steve Van Buren. Although he was a running back, he was bigger than most linemen of his day. Van Buren was not only powerful, he was very fast. He could run the 100-yard dash in under 10 seconds. Philadelphia's quarterback was Tommy Thompson. Thompson was blind in one eye, but he was one of the league's smartest players. If he found a weakness in the other team's defense, he would wait for just the right moment to strike.

Tommy Thompson

From 1944 to 1946, the Eagles finished second in the NFL's **Eastern Division** each year. In 1947, Philadelphia finished first, but lost to the Chicago Cardinals in the NFL

Steve Van Buren plows through tacklers (and the snow) for the
only touchdown of the 1948 championship game.

Championship. In 1948 and 1949, the team reached its peak.
During those two seasons, the Eagles lost just three games. They
scored 761 points and only allowed 290.

Philadelphia's great defense was at its best in the big games. In
the 1948 NFL Championship, the Eagles did not allow the
Cardinals to score. Van Buren, running the ball in a blinding
snowstorm, scored the only touchdown in a 7–0 victory. In the
1949 NFL Championship, against the Los Angeles Rams, a

rainstorm turned the field into a mud puddle. Van Buren ran through the muck for 196 yards, and the Eagles won 14–0.

The Eagles returned to the championship game in 1960. Their quarterback was Norm Van Brocklin. He was a great leader who was nearing the end of his playing days. Van Brocklin loved to throw the football. His favorite receivers were Tommy McDonald and Pete Retzlaff. They were equally good at catching short passes or long "bombs"—a Van Brocklin specialty.

CHUCK BEDNARIK
LINEBACKER   PHILADELPHIA EAGLES

Chuck Bednarik played linebacker and center for the 1960 Eagles.

The heart of the Philadelphia defense was Chuck Bednarik. He had been a young man on the championship teams of 1948 and 1949. Now he was one of the oldest players in the NFL. Bednarik was the Eagles' best linebacker, and also the team's center. He was the last true **two-way player** in football.

The Eagles met the Green Bay Packers in December of 1960 for the NFL Championship. Both teams had good defenses. The Eagles stopped Green Bay's runners, while the Packers kept Van Brocklin from **completing** passes. The Eagles led 10–6 at halftime, but the Packers scored at the beginning of the third quarter to take a 13–7 lead.

Philadelphia's Ted Dean received the kickoff and **returned** the ball to the Green Bay 39 yard line. Seven plays later, Dean carried it into the end zone to give the Eagles a 17–14 lead. The Packers made a furious comeback, but the Eagles stopped them on the 9 yard line. After the game, Van Brocklin and coach Buck Shaw announced that they were retiring.

Over the next 45 years, the Eagles had some wonderful players and

Norm Van Brocklin, the leader of the 1960 Eagles.

some excellent teams. They played the Oakland Raiders in Super Bowl XV and the New England Patriots in Super Bowl XXXIX, but lost both times. Despite the long wait, Philadelphia fans never gave up—and they never will. They remember the magical team that won the 1960 championship, and every season they believe the Eagles will find that magic again.

Go-To Guys

To be a true star in the NFL, you need more than fast feet and a big body. You have to be a "go-to guy"—someone the coach wants on the field at the end of a big game. Eagles fans have had a lot to cheer about over the years, including these great stars…

THE PIONEERS

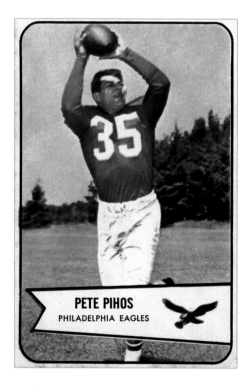

PETE PIHOS
PHILADELPHIA EAGLES

STEVE VAN BUREN — Running Back

- BORN: 12/28/1920
- PLAYED FOR TEAM: 1944 TO 1951

Steve Van Buren was nicknamed "Wham-Bam." He was one of the hardest men in history to tackle one-on-one.

PETE PIHOS — Receiver

- BORN: 10/22/1923
- PLAYED FOR TEAM: 1947 TO 1955

Pete Pihos had strong legs and sure hands, and he was an excellent **blocker**. Pihos also played defensive end for the Eagles.

CHUCK BEDNARIK · Linebacker/Center

- BORN: 5/1/1925 · PLAYED FOR TEAM: 1949 TO 1962

Chuck Bednarik was nicknamed "Concrete Charlie" because he was so tough. He was one of the last NFL stars to play offense and defense full-time.

NORM VAN BROCKLIN · Quarterback

- BORN: 3/15/1926 · DIED: 5/2/1983 · PLAYED FOR TEAM: 1958 TO 1960

In his three years with the Eagles, Norm Van Brocklin helped turn a losing team into NFL champions. He held players-only meetings every Monday morning so his teammates could discuss the previous day's game.

TOMMY MCDONALD · Receiver

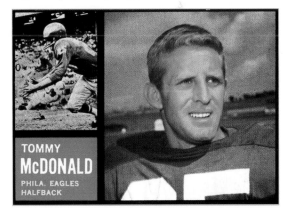

- BORN: 7/26/1934
- PLAYED FOR TEAM: 1957 TO 1963

Tommy McDonald was only 5' 9", but he played like a giant for the Eagles. He scored 67 touchdowns during his seven seasons in Philadelphia

HAROLD CARMICHAEL · Receiver

- BORN: 9/22/1949 · PLAYED FOR TEAM: 1971 TO 1983

At 6' 8", Harold Carmichael was one of the tallest receivers in football history—and one of the best. He ended his career as the Eagles' all-time leader in **receptions** (589), yards (8,978) and touchdowns (79).

LEFT: Pete Pihos   **ABOVE**: Tommy McDonald

MODERN STARS

WILBERT MONTGOMERY — Running Back

- BORN: 9/16/1954 • PLAYED FOR TEAM: 1977 TO 1984

Wilbert Montgomery could smash through the line for first downs or make long runs for touchdowns. He was one of the most feared and respected players in the NFL.

RON JAWORSKI — Quarterback

- BORN: 3/23/1951 • PLAYED FOR TEAM: 1977 TO 1986

Ron Jaworski was one of the smartest quarterbacks ever. When "Jaws" was running the offense, it was like having a second head coach on the field.

REGGIE WHITE — Defensive End

- BORN: 12/19/1961 • DIED: 1/6/2005 • PLAYED FOR TEAM: 1985 TO 1992

Reggie White was bigger, stronger, faster, and quicker than anyone else at his position. It took two or three blockers to keep him from **sacking** the quarterback. White was voted to the **Pro Bowl** 13 times in his career.

RANDALL CUNNINGHAM — Quarterback

- BORN: 3/27/1963 • PLAYED FOR TEAM: 1985 TO 1995

Randall Cunningham could throw an 80-yard touchdown pass, or run 80 yards for a touchdown. In 1990, he threw 30 touchdown passes and ran for almost 1,000 yards.

Brian Dawkins celebrates another Philadelphia victory.

BRIAN DAWKINS   Safety

• BORN: 10/13/1973   • FIRST SEASON WITH TEAM: 1996

When the Eagles **drafted** Brian Dawkins, they hoped he would turn into a dependable defensive player. He became something much more—a player who could sack the quarterback, tackle big running backs, and intercept passes.

DONOVAN MCNABB   Quarterback

• BORN: 11/25/1976   • FIRST SEASON WITH TEAM: 1999

The Eagles became a championship *contender* the day they made Donovan McNabb their starting quarterback. His football skills and leadership helped to make the team one of the most feared and respected in the NFL.

On the Sidelines

The Eagles have had some of the most important people in football walk their sidelines. Bert Bell, the team's first owner, was a brilliant man. When the NFL was struggling, he saw its great possibilities. Bell convinced the other team owners to evenly divide the best college players among each club. Today this process is called the NFL Draft. In 1946, Bell was named NFL commissioner.

The Eagles have also had some excellent coaches. "Greasy" Neale built the Eagles into champions during the 1940s. He created new defensive strategies to stop the passing game, and got his players to give 100 percent all the time. Buck Shaw, the coach of the 1960 championship squad, stressed the importance of team spirit. He made one of the NFL's worst teams into one of its best.

No Philadelphia coach was smarter, or more demanding, than Dick Vermeil. His team won the **National Football Conference (NFC)** championship in 1980 and went to Super Bowl XV. Under coach Buddy Ryan, the Eagles became known for their hard-hitting defense. The Eagles' next trip to the Super Bowl came in January of 2005, with Andy Reid on the sidelines. Reid found the right mix of offense and defense you need to win championships.

Fiery leaders like Andy Reid have made the Eagles winners.

One Great Day

At the beginning of each season, the goal of every NFL player is the same. Everyone wants to play in the Super Bowl. At the end of the 2001, 2002, and 2003 seasons, the Eagles reached the NFC title game. Each time, the team lost. Football fans were beginning to wonder if the Eagles would ever take that last, magical step.

After winning the most games in the NFC in 2004 and defeating the Minnesota Vikings in the first round of the **playoffs**, the Eagles found themselves in the championship game for the fourth year in a row. This time they would face the Atlanta Falcons and their dangerous quarterback, Michael Vick. A crowd of nearly 70,000 shivering fans took their seats at Lincoln Financial Field on a frigid, blustery day. The ***wind-chill factor*** made the temperature feel like -5°.

The Eagles scored first on a touchdown by Dorsey Levens, but the Falcons stormed back and reached Philadelphia's two yard line. Lineman Hollis Thomas saved the day when he sacked Vick, and the Falcons had to settle for a **field goal**. Each team scored a touchdown in the second quarter to make the score 14–10, Philadelphia.

The players knew what they had to do in the second half. The defense had to control the Falcons and the offense had to control the ball. The Eagles were magnificent over the final 30 minutes. Donovan McNabb played near perfect football, and the defense prevented the Falcons from scoring a single point. The final score was 27–10. The Eagles were NFC champions for the first time in 24 years!

Donovan McNabb and team owner Jeffrey Lurie celebrate Philadelphia's first trip to the Super Bowl since 1980.

Legend Has It

Was Bill Hewitt the NFL's most hard-headed player?

LEGEND HAS IT that he was. Hewitt starred for the Eagles from 1937 to 1939. During this time, most NFL players wore thick leather helmets to protect their heads. Hewitt refused to wear one until the league forced him to do so, in the 1940s. Luckily, all those blows to the head did not seem to affect him. Hewitt was a genius when it came to inventing **trick plays**.

Who was the best punter in team history?

LEGEND HAS IT that it was Randall Cunningham—a quarterback! Cunningham used his strong legs for running most of the time. But when Philadelphia's regular **punter** was hurt, he would kick for the team. Cunningham's booming kicks were legendary. In a 1989 game against the Giants, he launched one 91 yards. Five years later, he kicked an 80-yarder against the Dallas Cowboys.

What is the Eagles' most famous play?

LEGEND HAS IT that it was the "Miracle in the Meadowlands." On November 19, 1978, the Eagles trailed the New York Giants 17–12 at Giants Stadium, which is a part of the Meadowlands Sports Complex. The Giants had the ball with 20 seconds left, and the Eagles had used up all of their timeouts. New York needed to run one play to end the game and seal the victory. Quarterback Joe Pisarcik took the **snap** and tried to hand the ball to running back Larry Csonka. The ball fell to the ground, and Herman Edwards of the Eagles raced into the Giants' **backfield** and scooped up the **fumble**. He ran 26 yards into the end zone to give his team an incredible victory. The fans in the Meadowlands sat in stunned silence. In Philadelphia, the fans celebrated long into the night.

Joe Pisarcik of the Giants watches as Herman Edwards prepares to pick up the football.

It Really Happened

AL "Whitey" WISTERT

During the 1940s, many of the NFL's players joined the military to fight in World War II. During this time of hardships and shortages, everyone in America was asked to **conserve** resources. In 1943, the Eagles and the Pittsburgh Steelers agreed to combine their teams. This is impossible to imagine today, but at the time it made a lot of sense.

The "Steagles," as some fans called the new team, were able to put good players on the field, and also saved money on travel. They played four of their home games in Philadelphia and two in Pittsburgh. The coaches—"Greasy" Neale of the Eagles and Walt Kiesling of the Steelers—shared control of the team.

The leaders of the Philadelphia-Pittsburgh club included a pair of young linemen named Al Wistert and Vic Sears. After the war, they would star for the Eagles during their championship years. They blocked for running back Jack Hinkle, who finished the season with 571 **rushing** yards. Hinkle lost the rushing championship by only one yard to Bill Paschal.

Among the other talented players on the team were linemen Bucko Kilroy and Elbie Schultz, running back Ernie Steele, and quarterback Roy Zimmerman. Also on the "Steagles" was a left-handed quarterback named Allie Sherman. Sherman would become one of the NFL's best coaches during the 1960s.

The players on the Eagles and Steelers had been fierce rivals before 1943. But everyone worked together and beat some good teams, including the Washington Redskins, New York Giants, and Chicago Cardinals. The "Steagles" finished the season with five wins and a tie.

TOP: Vic Sears, who was voted one of the NFL's best linemen in 1943.
LEFT: Al Wistert, one of the top players on the "Steagles."

Team Spirit

When you play for the Eagles, you have to prove yourself every game. The fans make sure of that. The people in the stands at Eagles games may be the most *passionate* in all of football. When the team plays well, it is showered with love. When they play poorly, the fans really let them have it.

The Eagles want their fans to have fun at games. Their stadium has great views and an amazing sound system. The team mascot, Swoop the Eagle, is one of the most popular in the NFL. The Eagles' dance team entertains the fans during timeouts.

Of course, sometimes the fans make their own fun. In fact, Eagles fans are also famous for the wild costumes they wear to games. Every Sunday, they try to outdo one another. Sometimes the competition in the stands is as fierce as it is on the field!

You never know what you will see next at an Eagles game.

Timeline

In this timeline, each Super Bowl is listed under the year it was played. Remember that the Super Bowl is held early in the year, and is actually part of the previous season. For example, Super Bowl XL was played on February 4 of 2006, but it was the championship of the 2005 NFL season.

1939
The Eagles play Brooklyn in the first televised NFL game.

1960
The Eagles beat the Green Bay Packers for the NFL Championship.

1933
The Philadelphia Eagles play their first NFL season.

1948
The Eagles win their first NFL championship.

1949
The Eagles win their second NFL championship in a row.

Ed Matesic, the team's top passer in the mid 1930s

Harold
Carmichael

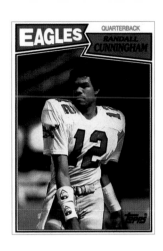

Randall
Cunningham

1973
Harold Carmichael
leads the NFL with 67
pass receptions.

1990
Randall Cunningham
is named NFL Player
of the Year.

1962
Eagles' quarterback
Sonny Jurgensen
leads the NFL in
passing.

1981
The Eagles reach
Super XV but lose
to the Raiders.

2005
The Eagles lose to
the Patriots in Super
Bowl XXXIX.

Donovan McNabb scrambles
away from tacklers during Super
Bowl XXXIX in February of 2005.

Fun Facts

SUNDAY BEST

Bert Bell bought the Eagles after learning that the city of Philadelphia was planning to allow sports to be played on Sundays. One of the reasons the Yellow Jackets lost money was because they had been forced to play on Saturdays, when most football fans were at college games.

SAFETY FIRST

In 1939, Philadelphia **rookie** Davey O'Brien led the NFL in passing. After the 1940 season—when the Eagles lost 10 of 11 games—he quit football to become an *FBI* agent. O'Brien said it was a safer job!

Bert Bell welcomes Davey O'Brien to the Eagles in 1939.

HOT FOOT

One of the best kickers in team history was Tony Franklin, who played for the Eagles from 1979 to 1983. Franklin kicked barefoot—no matter how cold or muddy the field was.

MOTHERLY LOVE

Donovan McNabb's mother, Wilma, became the most famous mom in the NFL. She appeared in a soup commercial with her son, and was so popular that she was made the star of the company's *ad campaign*.

THE START OF SOMETHING BIG

On October 22, 1939, the Eagles played in the first NFL game ever shown on television. They were playing the Dodgers in Brooklyn's Ebbets Field. Bill Hewitt caught a touchdown pass for the Eagles, but the star of the day was Ralph Kercheval. He kicked three long field goals for Brooklyn. There were fewer than 1,000 television sets in New

RALPH
KERCHEVAL

York City at the time. Those lucky enough to own one saw the Dodgers win 23–14. Today, NFL games are shown on television in more than 150 countries.

TOP: Wilma and Donovan McNabb   **ABOVE**: Ralph Kercheval

Talking Football

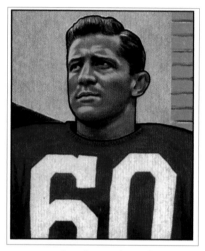

Chuck Bednarik

"I'm not one of the last 60-minute players. I am *the* last. I could do everything but eat a football."

—*Chuck Bednarik, on playing offense and defense*

"I played with a broken thumb. At one time or another every finger on my right hand was broken...I thought that was the way the game was played. You get knocked down, you get back up. Knocked down, get back up. I didn't consider it a badge of courage."

—*Ron Jaworski, on playing with pain*

"Yes, I've been booed. But I want the people of Philadelphia to know that when I don't get it done, I feel worse than the person who boos, because I've let myself down as well."

—*Randall Cunningham, on the importance of giving 100 percent*

Donovan McNabb

"I'm not worried about individual **accolades** or what people say about me. I'd rather people talk about the Eagles. I want to win the Super Bowl, and I want this team to be first in everything."

—*Donovan McNabb, on putting the team first*

"You hope to get guys to buy into what you're doing, to believe in the system. If you do that, you have a chance."

—*Andy Reid, on the secret to being a winning coach*

For the Record

The great Eagles teams and players have left their marks on the record books. These are the "best of the best"...

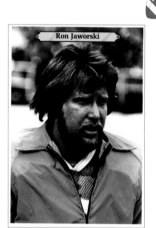

Ron Jaworski

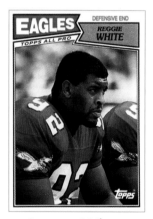

Reggie White

EAGLES AWARD WINNERS

WINNER	AWARD	YEAR
Greasy Neale	Coach of the Year	1948
Bobby Walston	Rookie of the Year	1951
Buck Shaw	Coach of the Year	1960
Norm Van Brocklin	Player of the Year	1960
Roman Gabriel	Comeback Player of the Year	1973
Dick Vermeil	Coach of the Year	1979
Ron Jaworski	Player of the Year	1980
Reggie White	Defensive Player of the Year	1987
Randall Cunningham	Player of the Year	1988
Keith Jackson	Rookie of the Year	1988
Randall Cunningham	Player of the Year	1990
Jim McMahon	Comeback Player of the Year	1991
Reggie White	Defensive Player of the Year	1991
Randall Cunningham	Comeback Player of the Year	1992
Ray Rhodes	Coach of the Year	1995
Andy Reid	Coach of the Year	2000
Andy Reid	Coach of the Year	2002

EAGLES ACHIEVEMENTS

ACHIEVEMENT	YEAR
NFL East Champions	1947
NFL Champions	1948
NFL Champions	1949
NFL Champions	1960
NFC East Champions	1980
NFC Champions	1980
NFC East Champions	1988
NFC East Champions	2001
NFC East Champions	2002
NFC East Champions	2003
NFC East Champions	2004
NFC Champions	2004

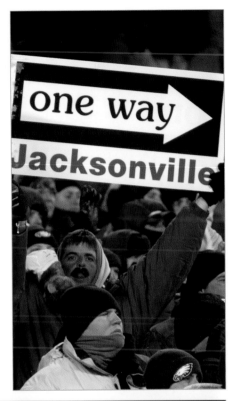

TOP: Eagles fans celebrate their trip to Super Bowl XXXIX in Jacksonville, Florida.
RIGHT: Dick Vermeil and Ron Jaworski discuss their next play during a game.

41

Pinpoints

T he history of a football team is made up of many smaller stories. These stories take place all over the map—not just in the city a team calls "home." Match the push-pins on these maps to the Team Facts and you will begin to see the story of the Eagles unfold!

TEAM FACTS

1 Philadelphia, Pennsylvania—*The team has played here since 1933.*

2 Bethlehem, Pennsylvania—*Chuck Bednarik was born here.*

3 Parkersburg, West Virginia—*Greasy Neale was born here.*

4 Chattanooga, Tennessee—*Reggie White was born here.*

5 Chicago, Illinois—*Donovan McNabb was born here.*

6 Green Bay, Wisconsin—*The Eagles won the 1960 NFL Championship here.*

7 Eagle Butte, South Dakota—*Norm Van Brocklin was born here.*

Steve Van Buren

8 Roy, New Mexico—*Tommy McDonald was born here.*

9 Los Angeles, California—*The Eagles won the 1949 NFL Championship here.*

10 New Orleans, Louisiana—*The Eagles played in Super Bowl XV here.*

11 Jacksonville, Florida—*Harold Carmichael was born here.*

12 Tela, Honduras—*Steve Van Buren was born here.*

Play Ball

Football is a sport played by two teams on a field that is 100 yards long. The game is divided into four 15-minute quarters. Each team must have 11 players on the field at all times. The group that has the ball is called the offense. The group trying to keep the offense from moving the ball forward is called the defense.

A football game is made up of a series of "plays." Each play starts and ends with a referee's signal. A play begins when the center snaps the ball between his legs to the quarterback. The quarterback then gives the ball to a teammate, throws (or "passes") the ball to a teammate, or runs with the ball himself. The job of the defense is to tackle the player with the ball or stop the quarterback's pass. A play ends when the ball (or player holding the ball) is "down." The offense must move the ball forward at least 10 yards every four downs. If it fails to do so, the other team is given the ball. If the offense has not made 10 yards after three downs—and does not want to risk losing the ball—it can kick (or "punt") the ball to make the other team start from its own end of the field.

At each end of a football field is a goal line, which divides the field from the end zone. A team must run or pass the ball over the goal line to score a touchdown, which counts for six points. After scoring a touchdown, a team can try a short kick for one "extra point," or try again to run or pass across the goal line for two points. Teams can score three points from anywhere on the field by kicking the ball between the goal posts. This is called a field goal.

The defense can score two points if it tackles a player while he is in his own end zone. This is called a safety. The defense can also score points by taking the ball away from the offense and crossing the opposite goal line for a touchdown. The team with the most points after 60 minutes is the winner.

Football may seem like a very hard game to understand, but the more you play and watch football, the more "little things" you are likely to notice. The next time you are at a game, look for these plays:

PLAY LIST

BLITZ—A play where the defense sends extra tacklers after the quarterback. If the quarterback sees a blitz coming, he passes the ball quickly. If he does not, he can end up on the bottom of a very big pile!

DRAW—A play where the offense pretends it will pass the ball, and then gives it to a running back. If the offense can "draw" the defense to the quarterback and his receivers, the running back should have lots of room to run.

FLY PATTERN—A play where a team's fastest receiver is told to "fly" past the defensive backs for a long pass. Many long touchdowns are scored on this play.

SQUIB KICK—A play where the ball is kicked a short distance on purpose. A squib kick is used when the team kicking off does not want the other team's fastest player to catch the ball and run with it.

SWEEP—A play where the ball-carrier follows a group of teammates moving sideways to "sweep" the defense out of the way. A good sweep gives the runner a chance to gain a lot of yards before he is tackled or forced out of bounds.

Glossary
FOOTBALL WORDS TO KNOW

ARTIFICIAL TURF—A playing surface made of plastic material, colored green to look like grass.

BACKFIELD—The area behind the blockers, where the quarterback and running backs start each play.

BLOCKER—A player who uses his body to protect the ball carrier.

COMMISSIONER—The person who runs a league. The NFL Commissioner is the head of the National Football League.

COMPLETING—Throwing a pass that is caught.

DRAFTED—Chosen from a group of the best college players.

EASTERN DIVISION—One of two groups of teams that made up the NFL between 1933 and 1949. The winners of the Eastern and Western Divisions played in the NFL Championship.

FIELD GOAL—A goal from the field, kicked over the crossbar and between the goal posts. A field goal is worth three points.

FUMBLE—A ball that is dropped by the player carrying it.

NATIONAL FOOTBALL CONFERENCE (NFC)—One of two groups of teams that make up the National Football League. The champion of the NFC plays the champion of the American Football Conference (AFC) in the Super Bowl.

NATIONAL FOOTBALL LEAGUE (NFL)—The league that started in 1920 and is still operating today.

NFL CHAMPIONSHIP—The game played each year to decide the winner of the league, from 1933 to 1969.

PLAYOFFS—The games played after the regular season that determine who plays in the Super Bowl.

PRO BOWL—The NFL's all-star game, played after the Super Bowl.

PROFESSIONAL—A person or team that plays a sport for money. College players are not paid, so they are considered "amateurs."

PUNTER—The player who kicks the ball to the other team after his team fails to make a first down.

RECEPTIONS—Passes that are caught.

RETURNED—Ran the ball back after a change of possession. The most common returns are punt returns, kickoff returns, and interception returns.

ROOKIE—A player in his first year.

RUSHING—Running with the football.

SACKING—Tackling the quarterback.

SNAP—The act of "hiking" the ball between the legs. The center snaps the ball into the quarterback's hands to start most plays.

STANDINGS—A daily list of teams, starting with the team with the best record and ending with the team with the worst record.

SUPER BOWL—The championship game of football, played between the winner of the American Football Conference (AFC) and National Football Conference (NFC).

TRICK PLAYS—Plays designed to fool an opponent. Trick plays can be very risky if they do not work.

TWO-WAY PLAYER—Someone who is on the field for both offense and defense for his team.

OTHER WORDS TO KNOW

ACCOLADES—Words of praise.

AD CAMPAIGN—A series of advertisements on television, radio, and in newspapers and magazines.

CONSERVE—Use slowly or protect.

CONTENDER—A person or team good enough to compete for a prize or championship.

EMERGE—Come out of.

FBI—The Federal Bureau of Investigation. This is the nation's main law enforcement agency.

GREAT DEPRESSION—A time of economic hardship during the 1930s.

PASSIONATE—Having strong emotions.

PLOTTED—Planned.

SUBURB—An area just outside a city.

TAILBONE—The bone that protects the base of the spine.

TALONS—The claws of a bird.

VETERANS—People who have experience doing a job.

WIND-CHILL FACTOR—The mathematical formula that estimates how much colder the air feels when it is windy.

Places to Go

ON THE ROAD

LINCOLN FINANCIAL FIELD
One Lincoln Financial Field Way
Philadelphia, PA 19148
(215) 463-2500

THE PRO FOOTBALL HALL OF FAME
2121 George Halas Drive NW
Canton, Ohio 44708
(330) 456-8207

ON THE WEB

THE NATIONAL FOOTBALL LEAGUE   www.nfl.com
  • *Learn more about the National Football League*

THE PHILADELPHIA EAGLES   www.Eagles.com
  • *Learn more about the Philadelphia Eagles*

THE PRO FOOTBALL HALL OF FAME   www.profootballhof.com
  • *Learn more about football's greatest players*

ON THE BOOKSHELF

To learn more about the sport of football, look for these books at your library or bookstore:

  • Ingram, Scott. *A Football All-Pro*. Chicago, IL.: Heinemann Library, 2005.

  • Kennedy, Mike. *Football*. Danbury, CT.: Franklin Watts, 2003.

  • Suen, Anastasia. *The Story of Football*. New York, NY.: PowerKids Press, 2002.

Index

PAGE NUMBERS IN **BOLD** REFER TO ILLUSTRATIONS.

The Team

MARK STEWART has written more than 20 books on football, and over 100 sports books for kids. He grew up in New York City during the 1960s rooting for the Giants and Jets, and now takes his two daughters, Mariah and Rachel, to watch them play in their home state of New Jersey. Mark comes from a family of writers. His grandfather was Sunday Editor of *The New York Times* and his mother was Articles Editor of *The Ladies Home Journal* and *McCall's*. Mark has profiled hundreds of athletes over the last 20 years. He has also written several books about New York and New Jersey. Mark is a graduate of Duke University, with a degree in history. He lives with his daughters and wife, Sarah, overlooking Sandy Hook, NJ.

JASON AIKENS is the Collections Curator at the Pro Football Hall of Fame. He is responsible for the preservation of the Pro Football Hall of Fame's collection of artifacts and memorabilia and obtaining new donations of memorabilia from current players and NFL teams. Jason has a Bachelor of Arts in History from Michigan State University and a Masters in History from Western Michigan University where he concentrated on sports history. Jason has been working for the Pro Football Hall of Fame since 1997; before that he was an intern at the College Football Hall of Fame. Jason's family has roots in California  and has been following the St. Louis Rams since their days in Los Angeles, California. He lives with his wife Cynthia in Canton, OH.